GOTHIC SCULPTURE

For description of frontispiece see back of title page

THE ACANTHUS HISTORY OF SCULPTURE

GENERAL EDITORS: SIR HERBERT READ, H. D. MOLESWORTH

GOTHIC SCULPTURE

THE INTIMATE CARVINGS

BY DR. MAX H. VON FREEDEN

Director of the Mainfränkisches Museum in Würzburg

PHOTOGRAPHED BY

F. L. KENETT

NEW YORK GRAPHIC SOCIETY
Arts & Books

PUBLISHED BY

NEW YORK GRAPHIC SOCIETY

GREENWICH, CONNECTICUT

FRONTISPIECE

Burial of Christ

French; late thirteenth century
Louvre, Paris

The carver's virtuosity and his delight in original composition
can be seen in the perfection of this outstanding group. Cour-
ageous determination and transfigured grief mark the face of
the figure bearing Our Lord, and the limpness of the corpse's
head is equally vivid. The golden borders of the carefully draped
garments give some idea of the original richness of this ivory.

PRINTED IN THE NETHERLANDS
by Joh. Enschedé en Zonen, Haarlem

Contents

Intimate Carvings by Dr. Max H. Von Freeden

The Plates

The Intimate Carvings

The thirteenth, fourteenth and fifteenth centuries, spanned by what we term the Gothic period, saw a revolution in the social and economic life of Europe. As princes created fixed capitals for themselves instead of the earlier uncomfortable peripatetic courts, so the earlier agricultural system gave way before a more modern money economy. Both movements brought great changes in their train and were to have a profound effect upon the arts.

For the first, the building of castles, palaces and town residences not only gave a new importance to the visual effect of surroundings but also to the ideas of comfort and luxury.

The court of Burgundy led the way and life came to be dominated by intricate ceremonial inherited in part from antiquity, Byzantium and the orient, and elaborated into an obligatory etiquette destined to reach its most exaggerated expression in baroque Spain. Something of this still prevails today in court and diplomatic protocol.

At the end of the period this court culture flowered into what was an almost decadent magnificence. Today this twilight of the Middle Ages is proverbially thought of in terms of banquets and hunts, ceremonial and knightly gatherings, tourneys or feasts which present a brilliant setting. But at the same time the indulgence of excessive lusts, sensuality, strange whims and gruesome sports found a place alongside the gastronomic orgies arrayed with crystal and gold plate. Palace halls were hung with richly figured tapestries and decorated with priceless furnishings. Superbly carved altars adorned the private chapels. Exquisite jewellery, caskets and miniatures all served their end. But the picture is incomplete without jesters and dwarfs as well as the artists and craftsmen.

At the beginning of the period we are still largely concerned with the achievements in ecclesiastical art and above all with architecture, which predominated.

In its transition from the Romanesque, Gothic architecture was characterized by an open stone framework supporting a stone vaulting. As this development reached its peak, painting and sculpture were almost completely subjected to architecture, though all three arts were ultimately to gain.

It was inevitable that large-scale mural painting should give way as the walls of Gothic churches were increasingly devoted to ever-larger windows. However, these new transparent walls of glass were quickly claimed by the painters and at the very moment when they were most dependent upon the good will of the architect, they achieved their greatest triumphs; for this new painting with colour and light on enormous areas of glass amounted to the conquest of a new artistic field. Glass painting, from being a pleasant accessory of the old order of architecture, had gradually become an indispensable feature of Gothic interior decoration. Its greatest successes were achieved, as were those of the Gothic style as a whole, primarily north of the Alps, and its decline accompanied that of the style as a whole.

In appropriating sculpture, Gothic cathedral architecture presented it with such gigantic new problems that it was taxed almost beyond its strength. The figures that had previously been sparingly applied to doorways and towers multiplied and became immense crowds nestling in groups round doorways and towers. As a result of this dependence on architecture, more sculpture was commissioned in the Gothic period than at any other time between antiquity and the baroque era; indeed the sculptor has probably never been so much in demand as he was then.

In addition, it was still the province of the sculptor to decorate church equipment and furniture. At a time when secular commissions were rare, sculpture became powerful in this "free" branch of its craft, and ventured into yet another field, that of monuments and tombs.

At the end of the Gothic period, when architecture tired, when cathedrals, started at the peak of the period, remained unfinished despite increasingly extended building periods; when towers, planned on a gigantic scale, were left incomplete; when niches on pillars and portals still remained empty, sculpture was still strong enough to leave the sinking ship, alert enough to recapture part of its former territory. It was altar-decoration which gave new life to the dying art of monumental sculpture. Here sculptors and wood carvers gradually developed the simplicity of the early retable into an architectural structure worthy to carry their figures. The Gothic winged altar grew from the *mensa*, until, high under the distant vaulting, multitudinous groups of figures were gathered into its forest-like branches, both over centrepiece and over wings.

The plates in this book are devoted to this independent sculpture and to carvings which were not tied to architecture or monumental decoration, and which may be described as free sculpture. Many indeed may be termed intimate sculptures. In so far as they are smaller than life size, and as they are independent of any monumental background, they appear more intimate and approachable than the larger works.

At the close of the Gothic period a true *Kleinplastik* developed – *Kleinplastik* is an untranslatable word which applies to small, delicate carvings, sometimes only a few inches high, which were later to become the passion of the lay collector with his delight in elaborate material and craftsmanship.

The larger pieces in this book were created to be seen in spacious halls or small chapels and there they might be set in places that obtained their feeble, dusky light through stained-glass windows. Those who stood before them had already left the real world at the door. To them, the human element in the Madonnas and devotional figures was no longer so significant; viewed in this half-real context, the sculptures became imbued with a spiritual quality which both donor and viewer sought.

These larger works were not then so sparsely distributed as they are in churches and museums today. In their threefold function of decorating buildings, tombs, and altars they covered and filled their allotted space to over-flowing. Except in the case of single devotional images, these works were often grouped in a decorative scheme illustrating a theological concept and involving several figures, for instance on an altar or its housing, on choir stalls or fonts or in the decoration of reliquaries. In the perspective of the overcrowded late Gothic altars, especially those of the North, the periodical additions in a medieval church presented a reasonable aesthetic whole. The isolation in which works of art are deliberately placed in churches and museums today is misleading when we consider their medieval profusion. The decimation of medieval works was often the result of a change in taste or of devotional approach. In some cases it was the aftermath of some natural catastrophe or war, such as has occurred all too often during the last six hundred years.

The age of chivalry, the twelfth and thirteenth centuries, represented the climax of the cultures of Germany, England and France. Poetry attained a rare brilliance; architecture and sculpture, as well as the crafts, enjoyed large-scale commissions. The social life round the emperor and at the royal courts, as well as in the castles of the feudal lords and amongst their tenants, blossomed into magnificent splendour, transfigured by the heritage of the Orient, whose treasures, sciences and customs were introduced into Europe by the returning crusaders.

With the Hohenstaufen emperors the medieval concept of imperial sovereignty flourished for the last time before disintegrating in the stormy conflict between imperial and papal power. In the kingdoms of the West, a sense of national consciousness was awakening but was kept in check by a common faith, by strong cultural ties arising out of commonly held aims, and, most of all, by the bond that united all countries: the crusades.

From modest roots poetry soon flowered. Chronicles, songs, proverbs and poems came into being, generally in the service of courtly love. Rhymed moral precepts tell us a great deal about the burgeoning social life. All this was brought into focus by the minstrels, who wandered from castle to castle, welcome wherever they went.

The lyrical nature poems and love songs of the troubadours spread north-wards from the south of France where they originated, and the martial vigour of the poems of Bertran de Born was softened by the form which came to be known in Germany as *Minnesang*. Literary monuments of this period are the *Tristan* of Gottfried von Strassburg, the *Parzival* of Wolfram von Eschenbach, and the lyrics of Walter von der Vogelweide. The architectural legacy of the epoch is still to be seen in its buildings – its cathedrals, its abbeys and its castles.

The ideals of the thirteenth century were still those that had inspired the crusades and which, towards the end of the eleventh century, had fired the western Christian world with a zeal to free the Holy Land from the Mohammedan infidels. In the space of a few generations, religious fervour and love of adventure moved hundreds of thousands from every country to do battle with the dangerously advancing forces of Islam. Great victories awaited them, but also shameful defeats; fame and riches, but imprisonment and miserable death as well.

As late as the middle of the thirteenth century, France's pious king and saint, Louis IX, to whom we owe the Sainte Chapelle in Paris, undertook another crusade, sailing to Cyprus with over forty thousand soldiers. In 1270 he went on the last crusade, to Tunis. Palestine was soon lost, town by town, and by 1291 the Christian conquerors had evacuated the country, to return only as pilgrims. Against this failure of two hundred years' struggle with the Near East we must place the permanent successes for Christianity in Spain and eastern Europe and, for the Church itself, in the founding of the orders of the Christian Knights. Furthermore for the generations of crusaders the first contact with what was to them a new world – the Orient – had a lasting effect. It provided a cultural stimulus without which neither the high flowering of these centuries nor the achievements of the ensuing period can be understood.

Europeans of different lands, and speaking different languages, had fought together for the common faith; they had come to know one another in military camps, and had discovered that they shared common ties of faith, custom and culture. This epoch brought into being a new international class side by side with the clergy – the brotherhood of the Christian Knights. An aristocracy of the sword with strong family and cultural ties arose out of this common experience, and remained a powerful bond between countries for generations, even for centuries.

On the other hand the yeomen, who had formed a large section of the population and who had enjoyed some importance through the tenure of land, began to lose significance. With the growth of the cities, however, a new class came into being – the burghers. In the following centuries, they were to overtake the feudal aristocracy by their superior economic power and also, in certain cases, by their greater cultural force.

An important after-effect of the period of the crusades, which really ended at the close of the thirteenth century, was the growing prosperity, not only at the courts but also amongst the lesser nobility and the burghers. It was accompanied by a taste for luxury, a desire for a less simple mode of life, which in turn generated the forces needed to satisfy the new demands. The world had become, in contemporary eyes, not only bigger and wider, but also more beautiful and interesting. Thus poetry and the arts, as well as the crafts, which had worked almost solely for the honour of God and the glory of his Church, were now called upon to glorify the everyday world.

Commerce and the crafts, in all their colourful diversity, gained respect. As they grew in importance, guilds and merchant companies came into being, and succeeded in getting a voice in the administration of the cities, until the cities finally obtained freedom from the feudal overlord, owed allegiance only to the emperor, and were able to form political alliances with other cities. There was no more bondage for the burgher. The main roads met in the cities, which were the centres for travellers and pilgrims and for the trade of goods from far and near. The great building organizations were situated within their walls and they sheltered the artists and craftsmen; new wealth accumulated in the cities and with it a new civic pride appeared.

All these developments offered the Gothic sculptor and carver many opportunities and, moreover, each generation had an insatiable desire to express its own artistic feeling. This was only made possible, over the years, by making room, by repeatedly clearing away or destroying the "outmoded" work of previous generations. One example, which will serve for many, occurred in Würzburg in 1493 when Riemenschneider put an *Adam and Eve* above the market gate of the *Marienkapelle:* to enable him to do so, the town council removed the statues of the first man and woman that were already standing there, even though they had been erected only two generations earlier.

Furthermore, the changing and often more elaborate liturgical customs and rites of the high and late Middle Ages demanded new equipment, new furnishings, and these afforded new subjects for the artist. For example, the appearance of the Rosary brotherhoods of the late Middle Ages produced a flood of Gothic Madonnas. The fast-spreading cult of St Anne led to the creation of charming groups showing her with the Virgin and Child.

The number of altars increased considerably during the Gothic period in the cathedrals and collegiate churches especially, but also in the parish churches. The spacious churches of this era often had dozens of altars, sometimes more than fifty. The burgher, noble, or even ecclesiastic donors of these altars made themselves responsible for the material needs of the priest who served at their altar as well as for the provision of an artistically conceived altar with furnishings of admirable craftsmanship. For such an altarpiece tradition demanded a representation of the patron saint, a cross, candelabra, an altar cloth, and robes. The buttresses of the new churches favoured the construction of subsidiary chapels and thereby increased the potential space for additional altars, which meant more commissions for the artists.

The altarpiece which, as the chief domain of art, combined painting and sculpture in a common effort, has become the classic expression of late Gothic art for the world at large. In these altarpieces, the central section was generally reserved for three-dimensional figures. The insides of the wings were often given to the carvers for their reliefs, if they had not already been allotted to the painters – for whom the outsides of the wings were always reserved. Such an altar complex was indeed imposing; its changing face – different on weekdays, Sundays and feast days – served as a kind of three-dimensional picture book of the church year for a pious world which could as yet neither read nor write, and so readily sought these vivid illustrations of the scriptures.

It was characteristic of the age to take pleasure in distinctions of rank and prestige, however small, and this gave rise to a new kind of church furniture: the special seats for high and low priesthood, for landlord and councillor. In the Middle Ages the common people used to stand through the services; only later, with the Counter Reformation, were the pew and the confessional introduced.

Towards the end of the Middle Ages the fixed pulpit became significant as a focal point inside the church, as did the tabernacle. The latter started as a simple wall cupboard, but grew, as did the altar with its superstructure and the pulpit with its sounding board, to afford yet another opportunity for more decorative figures which became ever more elaborately carved. The patrons' delight in ornament was so great and the artists' delight in narrative so insatiable that it was an effort for scholars to devise a constant flow of theological subjects suitable for them to work on.

The rood loft and choir-screen widely used in the Romanesque period, later became indispensable in almost all cathedrals and abbeys. They separated transept and nave from the choir, which was often extended for the growing number of participants in the liturgy, and they also excluded the congregation both spatially and visually. No longer able to see anything of the ceremonies being enacted at the high altar, the congregation were given a new, second altar.

Gothic sculpture, like Gothic architecture, originated in France, and it, too, spread rapidly throughout Europe, varying in each country. Gothic art had become common to all of Europe, and its national variants did not develop in isolation, although they always remained distinct within the framework of the style. There was a good deal of practical exchange, and German holy images were ordered from and sent to Italy, French ivory caskets and small altars were exported to England and Germany and English alabasters were exported throughout Europe.

The sculpture of the early thirteenth century was often filled with an exuberant, festive spirit. Its creations radiated joy, and were visibly living in that serene, harmonious unity between earthly and heavenly existence which poetry tells us should be the aim of life.

With the approach of the fourteenth century, religious interest in the next world increased, until the thought of death as the real aim of life grew more prevalent and more clearly defined. Life on earth became nothing more than an obstacle in the path towards the desired afterlife. This feeling must have been intensified as a result of the terrible plagues in the middle of the century, in the course of which a very large proportion of the population of Europe died.

But the pendulum swung back again. With the dawning of the fifteenth century the attitude to life once more became affirmative, and the forms in which it was expressed became naturalistic. At the end of the Gothic era sculpture was finally allowed expression either in ornamental exaggeration or in a new inner intensity.

The early Gothic figure was, in fact, conceived altogether sculpturally and occupied an independent position alongside painting. Figure compositions, too, grew out of a truly plastic imagination. Soon a linear element crept in to heighten feeling and mood. The typical S-shaped curves of the standing figures combined plastic and linear elements.

Towards the end of the period, we find in Germany a tendency to regard the animation of dead matter as the ultimate goal of sculpture and to achieve this through an elaborate use of line. This perhaps reflects a more complex view of man as something other than a simple child of nature. In France the treatment of the drapery was never permitted completely to obscure the human form.

The Western world found, in Gothic art, a means of symbolizing the Christian capacity to experience life and religion as conceived within the framework of medieval piety. Although each nation added something of its own national peculiarities the style retained its validity as a common artistic expression of Western Christianity and was universally recognized.

Whereas at the beginning the leading centres were the cathedral works of France, towards the end of the era the workshops of Swabia and Bavaria had gained the lead. Yet however much the Gothic style changed with time or varied locally, the overriding desire to adhere to a universal style was never absent.

At the climax of the Gothic period, which occurred about midway, the focus of patron and artist alike, whether in thought or in creative work, was not on this world: It was simply on God. Both thought and art were directed on the next world: this yearning for the unreal dominated the art of the time. A mystical retreat from the world, rather than a demand for true reality, accompanied the beginning of the Gothic style and its early flowering. Thus it honoured living nature as the work of divine creation, and took greedily whatever it needed from nature for its paintings and miniatures or for the decoration on its doorways and arches. Local plants and animals are to be found in the ornamentation of churches, palaces, town halls and guild halls.

So profoundly was the period absorbed by the doctrine of sin and mankind's sinful desires that people sought to compensate for their unworthiness by pious and charitable foundations of vast proportions. For medieval people, Man – whom God had made in his own image – was nevertheless not seen as the master of his world, but as a poor sinner, full of humility.

But in the Gothic period human beauty could only be seen in so far as it reflected divine creation. The artists were not interested in sensual warmth; even when they did not despise this quality they had no wish to represent the magic of physical perfection, which they viewed as purely the reflection of a pious soul.

Medieval art had wide didactic significance. It was a visual commentary on the Bible for the believer who could not read and was an aid to preaching which offered an opportunity for artistic creation.

At this time the theme and subject of the artist's commission were defined (uncommissioned work as such was still unknown). The artist was free to express himself only in his manner of presentation, and in this way period and personal styles developed, for here he could reveal both his personal style and that of his time.

The incentives to artistic creation lay in the patron's pious spirit or his desire for decorative objects. The styles changed in character according to an historical pattern, but this has only recently been defined by modern research.

This freedom of style was, of course, the only one the medieval artist possessed – valuable enough, but by twentieth-century standards rather limited; for the rest the artist was compelled to belong to a corporation, either to one of the great constructional organizations or to a guild, if he was not living within an ecclesiastical community. In his choice of themes he was almost entirely tied to religious subjects. Only after a long interval do wider themes from literature, myth, and history appear and only as the period draws to a close do conditions governing artistic creation become considerably freer.

As the fourteenth century turned from architecturally dominated sculpture towards independent works, the size of the figures diminished and there was a marked preference for work that was smaller than life-size. The smaller scale increased the sculptor's courage to experiment with new forms and content, and a comparable phenomenon is noticeable in the allied field of miniature painting. The growing preoccupation with the diminutive opened up many new possibilities. The group composition could develop, and the single devotional figure be essayed.

By this time the carver's (as opposed to the mason's) workshop tended to become established in one place though the master may have had his prescribed apprentice years of wandering behind him. His works, however, were to be found far from his home and they attracted new commissions from abroad. On the other hand, the building organizations were forced, by their very nature, to remain mobile. Their constituent members may have come from afar, and they moved, with their master, to wherever a building was needed. Where both groups, the sculptor-masons and the carvers, happened to be active in the same town, fruitful exchange and even competition might arise, especially in the new field of tomb making.

By the middle of the fifteenth century it was clear to whom the future in important sculpture belonged; the mason was the loser. From now on he was limited to work on architectural decoration and detail. The important statues were ordered from the carver.

Artists who, like some of today's sculptors, worked in both stone and wood bore witness to the invasion of the carver into the stonemason's domain. The stonemasons were not members of the carvers' guilds, though these welcomed the painters to whom the wings of the carved altars were often left, the glass painters, as well as the joiners whom the carver needed for the altar housing, and above all, the *Fassmaler*, who painted the sculptures. In some cases one man could be a carver and a painter: such a man was allowed to paint his own figures, or to supply the paintings for the wings of the altars he himself had carved.

Stone was the favourite, though not the only, raw material for sculpture in the early Gothic period. Where wood was used, it was treated like stone. Gradually wood, which was easier to work and which permitted a wider range of effects, achieved greater popularity. In the interim, clay and even artificial stone were used, for their stylistic possibilities. By the end of the period the position was reversed, and the stone sculptures often bore marked characteristics of wood carving. This is particularly noticeable for example in Riemenschneider's stone *Apostles*. In rare cases wood carvings replaced stone ornament on the façades of buildings, and thus invaded architecture itself, which had been the very sanctuary of stone.

The fourteenth century saw a great increase in the number of single sculptured figures not specifically designed to fit into an architectural scheme. The new religious outlook with its more intimate approach called for single figures suited to personal devotion at home as opposed to those used in church. Here the artist could create more freely, since the works did not have to fit into a theological scheme. Indeed the new challenge forced him to fresh invention.

Turning from the petrified prayer of cathedral sculpture and the hieratic, inflexible dogmas of high Gothic, the heart and eye of the believer could now meet and commune with his own patron saint. Also he could now afford to play the patron, to commission his own devotional figure, even if he was only a burgher, a master craftsman, or a merchant.

With the new development of the devotional object, as a single figure or as a group, the age created new subjects which were drawn up from the depths of popular piety into the light of the altar candles. Legends from the holy story which cannot be found in the scriptures were adopted as subject matter for works in wood and stone. These imaginative projections, based on details of the Passion, brought the beholder into close, almost personal, contact with the holy personages. These were, first and foremost, the group of Christ and St John and the *Pietà;* also represented were God the Father sitting with the crucified Christ and a dove, the Entombment with its many figures, and single figures such as the Man of Sorrows.

In revolt against the monumental, the emphasis was now on the small: the worshipper loved the intimate, the personal. He did not wish to be overpowered by his encounter with God, as in the great cathedral, but rather to approach him calmly in a small chapel or alone in front of his devotional figure.

New intentions give rise to new methods. The smaller format went with materials that were lighter and easier to work such as alabaster and clay; neither were new, of course, but clearly both appealed to the craftsman. The former, when freshly quarried, is still so soft that it can be worked with a knife. The latter, in its original state, is entirely formless, and is ideal for sketches and for experimental work on a small scale.

Alabaster hardens quickly when exposed to the air and is durable. Clay can be hardened either by drying or by firing.

Ivory, which had come through Byzantium to the West and had been popular for centuries, became easier to obtain after the crusades. Its soft, melting whiteness was found to be especially pleasing as taste became more refined and art came to be appreciated for its own sake apart from its religious significance.

When working on such a small scale with such pliable material there was always the danger of mannerism, or at least a mannered style – a danger which also arose in later centuries.

Ivory carving was mainly confined to France, which supplied England, Germany and the rest of Europe, while carving in alabaster was largely carried on in England and Germany, and exported to the other countries.

The fashion for small scale work spread by degrees to architectural sculpture, and thus architectural and "free" sculpture grew closer to each other again. Masons and carvers worked together on the larger long-term projects. The busily writing *Seated Apostles* (dating from about 1400), on the Minster at Ulm are a striking example of the almost playful, intimate style introduced at the turn of the century. Even more daringly life-like are the eight small figures who sit by the octagonal tower of the Minster in Strasbourg, looking up to the spire that was never to be completed. Formally they are still part of the cathedral sculpture; in spirit, however, they are no longer part of any religious programme, but the personification of onlookers watching any building operation. In the second half of the fourteenth century it was still new and exciting to find the Emperor Charles IV and the Empress bowing to the public from the balcony of a church in Thuringia *in stone;* just as, much later in rococo Bavaria, we find a stucco duke and duchess doing the same. This fresh and daring attempt to involve the casual onlooker in direct contact with the sculpture is more than mere drollery.

The fifteenth century brought further developments to the use of the single figure. Artistic appreciation was no longer confined to princes, dukes, and knights: the rich burghers and the craftsmen also left their mark as patrons, for they wanted to see their guild badges or family crests incorporated in the statues they had given to the churches and chapels.

By this time it was not only the apprentice who customarily travelled abroad in his youth. The works of the master craftsman, commissioned from afar, also travelled in their turn. Miniature altars and ivory caskets were ordered from foreign lands, and huge altars were commissioned by ambitious art lovers and sent abroad. The most impressive examples of these exports are to be found even today in the churches and museums around the Baltic sea coast, evidence of the regular export of late Gothic sculpture which made its way from N. Germany and the Low Countries to Scandinavia and elsewhere.

As we have said, not all the statues which stand as single figures in churches and art collections today were originally created as such. We must remember that the baroque period in particular had no sympathy with the Gothic, and that the very word "Gothic" became synonomous with "barbaric". A baroque altar might often be erected only at the expense of its medieval predecessor. And then, perhaps, individual statues which had won a place in the hearts of the worshippers, or which were reputed to work miracles, might be removed from groups of statuary, and re-erected elsewhere. Later these were often sold and thus found their way to some private or public collection.

Yet we can be grateful for these and for the sculptures which still remain in their original settings for the insight they afford into one of the most fascinating periods of Western art.

Grateful thanks are due to the Directors and staff of the Bayerisches Nationalmuseum, Munich; Ehem. Staatliche Museen, Berlin; Staatliche Museen, Berlin; Louvre, Paris; Landesmuseum, Bonn and the Victoria and Albert Museum, London for their help and permission to take the photographs.

PLATE 1

Mourning Virgin

German (Upper Saxony); c. 1220
Height: 65 inches
Ehem. Staatliche Museen, Berlin

This oak statue of the Virgin from Naumburg is the only figure remaining of a group of three. The crucified Christ was originally in the centre and John the Evangelist on his other side. The paint is old, but not original. The sorrow in the Virgin's face and the cloth pressed to her cheek convey the deep sense of mourning, but the position of the raised right hand, with the palm facing outwards, suggests restraint even in grief.

PLATE 2

Seated Christ or an Apostle

Lorraine (probably Nikolaus von Verdun); c. 1200
Height: 9¼ inches
Ehem. Staatliche Museen, Berlin

The quiet, contemplative air and monumental dignity of this bronze figure are typical of the work of craftsmen in the district of the Rhine and the Maas during the transition from Romanesque to Gothic at the end of the twelfth and beginning of the thirteenth centuries.

PLATES 3, 4

The Soissons Diptych

French; late thirteenth century
Height: 12¾ inches
Victoria and Albert Museum, London

This diptych from the cathedral of Soissons is the most important of a notable group of French ivories to which it has given its name. The scenes showing the Passion of Christ, grouped architecturally, present a beautifully decorative whole. The extreme subtlety of the carving is manifest in the detail of the Deposition from the Cross.

PLATE 4

The Soissons Diptych

See plate 3

4

PLATE 5

Christ and St John

German (Upper Swabia); c. 1320
Height: 35 inches
Ehem. Staatliche Museen, Berlin

Christ inclines his head towards the smaller figure of the sleeping Evangelist, and has placed his left hand tenderly on the latter's shoulder. Their right hands are lightly clasped together. Carved in oak, the statues still bear the original paint: the robes and cloaks are gilt, the latter lined with red; Christ's hair is dark brown, while the Evangelist's is lighter.

The groups of Christ and Saint John, which are really a detail of the Last Supper, were often shown out of their original context, and became a symbol of mystical union with Our Lord; as a devotional group, they were especially popular in convents in Swabia in the beginning of the fourteenth century.

PLATE 6

Virgin and Child

French; early fourteenth century
Height: 16 inches
Victoria and Albert Museum, London

This ivory statuette is one of the most delightful existing examples from a period noted for its grace and charm. It still shows traces of its original paint. The base is modern. The elegant inclination of the figure is characteristic of ivories of the period and derives from the natural curve of the tusk.

PLATES 7, 8

The Röttgen Pietà

German (Middle Rhine); c. 1370
Height: 10¼ inches (without base)
Rheinisches Landesmuseum, Bonn

As this group shows, working on a small scale enabled the artist to portray, and encouraged, an intensification of expression, which in Germany often took a terrifying and gruesome form. The artist has scorned conventional treatment in order to startle the beholder and convey the anguish of this moment. The countenance of the Virgin is transfigured with pain; drops of blood welling from Christ's five wounds and the rigidity of his arms and head portray his suffering. The fact that the dead body is smaller than that of Mary adds to the impact.

PLATE 8

The Röttgen Pietà

See plate 7

PLATE 9

Pastoral staff

French; first half of fourteenth century
Height: 5 inches
Victoria and Albert Museum, London

Within the circle of the crook, with its vine-leaf decoration, the Virgin and Child are seen enthroned between angels. The flat circular surface has been used with enormous skill to portray in depth a group of inimitable charm and decorative elegance. The fashionable and expensive ivory would have been regarded as well suited to episcopal rank and dignity.

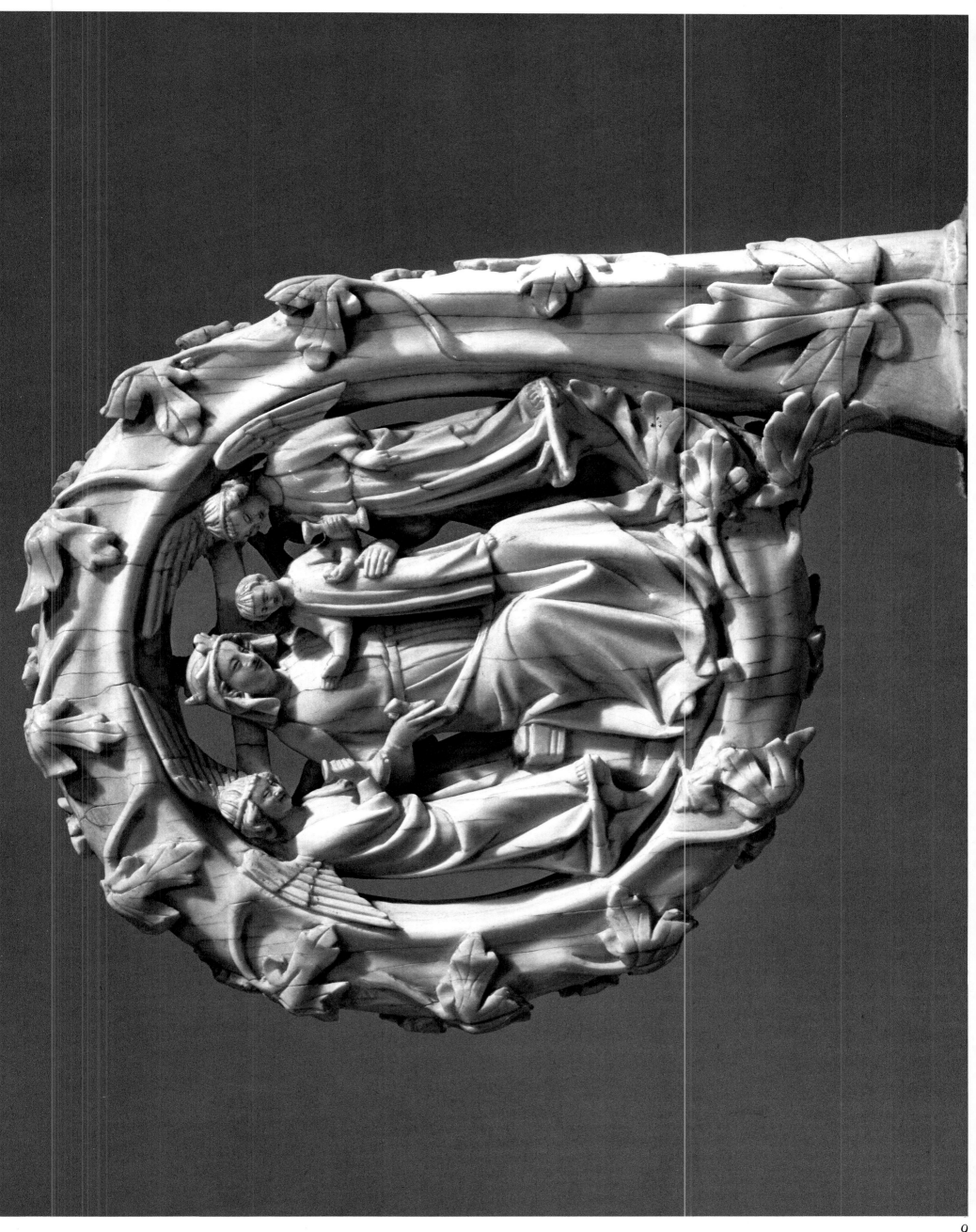

PLATE 10

Aquamanile in the form of a lion

North German; c. 1420
Height: 13¾ inches
Bayerisches Nationalmuseum, Munich

Throughout the Gothic period the vessels used by the priest
during Mass for the ritual washing were often given animal
shapes, notably those of the griffin and the lion, as in this
bronze example. Contemporary delight in the fabulous and
grotesque encouraged designs in which the medieval preoccupation with symbolism could combine with an unfettered
delight in sheer fantasy.

PLATE 11

Mirror case

French; first half of the fourteenth century
Diameter: 4⅞ inches
Victoria and Albert Museum, London

This mirror case is an article of pure luxury intended for court use. It shows the spontaneous delight with which the Parisian ivory carvers turned to secular themes; in this case a scene from the daily life of the nobility.

A knight and his lady are shown riding to the hunt, accompanied by two servants on foot. In the background, a wood is suggested, while in the foreground a dog chases a hare. The charm of chivalry is caught in the proud carriage of the horses, the tender smiles and gestures of the couple, and the happy faces of their followers.

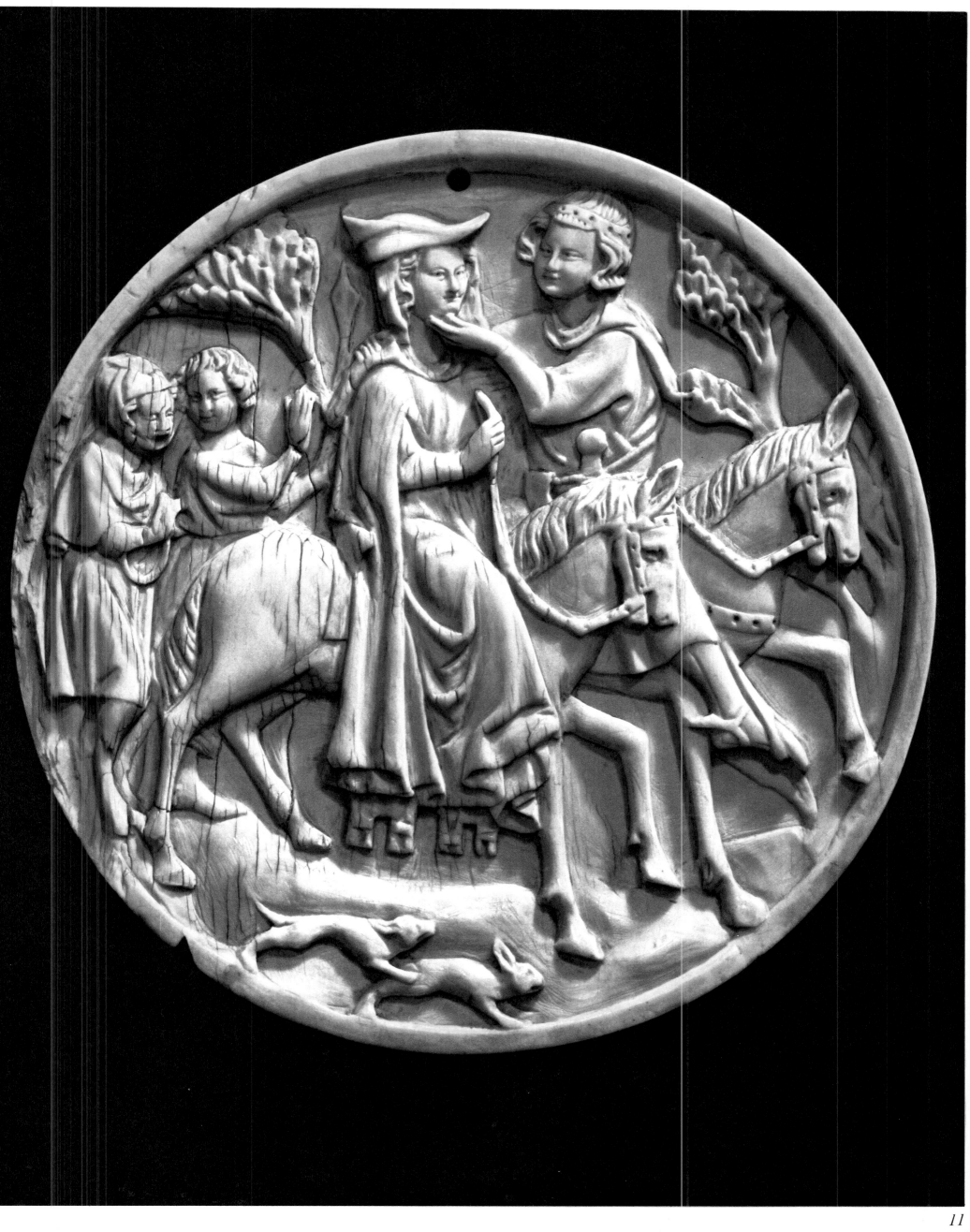

PLATE 12

Three Mourning Women

German (Upper Swabia); c. 1420
Height 45¾ inches
Staatliche Museen, Berlin

This limewood group by the Master of Biberach shows the fainting Mary supported by two mourning women. The rich harmonious beauty of the figures and the soft folds of their robes temper the expression of anguish and despair.

Pietà

German (Salzburg); c. 1420–30
Height: 29½ inches
Bayerisches Nationalmuseum, Munich

Carved in stone and with its original paint, this is among the most remarkable of the Pietàs. It came from a monastery at Seeon in Upper Bavaria. The lyrical style of this type of composition originated in the early fifteenth century and spread quickly; it probably reflects Bohemian influence. It is in strong contrast to the earlier figure (plate 7) in the softer handling of the expression, which is reflected in the folds of the drapery.

PLATE 14

Pietà

See plate 13

St Michael

German (Passau); c. 1490
Height: 48½ inches
Bayerisches Nationalmuseum, Munich

This limewood figure (which has lost its original paint) shows the youthful saint, with features of almost feminine beauty, standing on a dragon with the head of a dog and the horns of a ram. Saint Michael wears his ornamented armour elegantly; although poised to strike, his sword is held almost coquettishly behind his head while he fastidiously raises the tip of his cloak. This type of almost theatrical exaggeration became increasingly popular at this time. The artist is from the same district as the Master of Kefermarkt.

PLATE 23

St Michael

See plate 22

PLATE 24

St Christopher

German (Bavarian); c. 1480
Height: 9¼ inches
Ehem. Staatliche Museen, Berlin

The saint is shown wading barefoot through the water with the infant Christ on his shoulder. The Child is toying with his hair. The intimacy of conception coupled with the elaborate stylization of the drapery which billows upwards as if blown by the wind, is typical of Gothic carving as it moves into the sixteenth century.

Representations of Saint Christopher – sometimes of gigantic size – were to be found in nearly every Gothic church because of his reputed power to protect from sudden death anyone who contemplated his image daily. This painted lime-wood statuette may be one of a series depicting the "Fourteen Helpers" another cult which became increasingly popular after the middle of the fifteenth century. As perhaps in this case, these figures became a favourite subject for late Gothic altars where great numbers of saints could be placed in the wings or in the housing.

Two scenes from the Legend of St George

North French or Flemish; c. 1500
Height: 13⅜ inches
Victoria and Albert Museum, London

In the first of these carvings taken from an elaborate boxwood group the knightly saint is riding to battle, wearing a full suit of armour of the latest fashion. The next depicts the battle with the dragon, which emerges from a rocky cave, belching fire while the princess waits and prays in the background. The mythical monster is treated with every elaboration of Gothic ornament. The whole shows a winding hill rising to a castle at the summit. The various incidents are presented simultaneously. The anonymous artist shows an obvious delight in the theatrical and in the great elaboration of detail sought by the rich collectors of the time.

PLATE 26

Two scenes from the Legend of St George

See plate 25

PLATE 27

St Sebastian

South German (Upper Swabia); c. 1490
Height: 39 inches
Ehem. Staatliche Museen, Berlin

The precision of this limewood carving transmutes the bitter suffering of martyrdom into the passionate plea of the saint and as such creates a work of powerful intimacy and moving realism.

PLATE 28

Virgin and Child

German (Franconia); c. 1515
Height: 47⅜ inches
Ehem. Staatliche Museen, Berlin

This figure by the outstanding master of the late German
Gothic, Tilman Riemenschneider, typifies the intimate humanity of the sculptures of the time. Less ruggedly of the people
than the model for plate 31, the Madonna betrays the gentle
grace of an ordinary woman while the child playing with the
corner of her veil would have recalled a sight common to every
beholder of the time.

PLATES 29, 30

Zebedee and Mary Salome

German (Franconia); c. 1506
Height: 44½ inches, 8½ inches, 7½ inches
Victoria and Albert Museum, London

These limewood figures are fragments of a "family altar" by Tilman Riemenschneider. In the late fifteenth century it became increasingly popular to depict Christ's family in groups of several figures. These groups in the new realistic style gave the craftsman opportunity to portray people of various ages and types. Riemenschneider's intimate, thoughtful style and the basic lyricism of his art are readily appreciated and the brilliance of the carving is apparent.

PLATE 30

Zebedee and Mary Salome

See plate 29

Virgin and Child

German (Salzburg); c. 1430
Height: 42½ Width: 33⅛ inches
Bayerisches Nationalmuseum, Munich

This limewood group of the Virgin and Child from the monastery at Seeon in Upper Bavaria is in excellent condition and the original paint is outstandingly well preserved. The crown is gilt, set with coloured stones; the Virgin has golden hair and an enamel-white face with pink cheeks. She wears a white head cloth, and the lining of her gold cloak is glazed in red on a gold background. The bench and cushions are green; the carpet is gold and silver.

This carving is an outstanding example of the early fifteenth century movement towards a gentle and intimate treatment of religious figures. Its charm is particularly emphasized by the felicitous combination of form and colour and the heavy folds of the drapery add to its simple dignity.

PLATE 16

Head of John the Baptist

English; c. 1430
Height: 6½ inches
Bayerisches Nationalmuseum, Munich

This alabaster head, with its slightly open eyes and open mouth, gives an awesome impression of death. The carving is typical of the alabaster work produced in England and also to some degree in Northern France and the Netherlands. The material permitted of very easy handling and was extensively used for altarpieces and figures designed for export. It was virtually mass produced.

PLATE 17

The Virgin and Child with St Anne

Alsace; c. 1467
Height: 25½ inches
Staatliche Museen, Berlin

The group of the Virgin and Child with Saint Anne by Nicolaus Gerhaert von Leyden in red sandstone comes from Wissembourg in Alsace. The drapery treated in generous and increasingly elaborate folds is typical of the developments of the middle of the century.

One of the earliest known works by Nicolaus von Leyden, it shows the strong influence of the Burgundian tradition.

PLATE 18

Angel with the Infant Jesus

German (Bavaria-Swabia); about 1480
Height: 27¾ inches
Bayerisches Nationalmuseum, Munich

The unusual theme of this charming late Gothic group from the Ursuline Convent at Landsberg am Lech is drawn from the representations of " The Garden of Paradise " and is typical of the increasing humanity of the devotional approach in convents of the period.

The limewood group shows an angel supporting the Infant Jesus, who is taking his first steps. The body of the Child is painted flesh colour, and his rosary is red; the hair and robe of the angel are gilt, but the hair of the Child was removed at a later date, probably in order to set a crown on his head.

PLATE 19

The Virgin and Child: *The Dangolsheim Madonna*

Alsace; c. 1470
Height: 40⅛ inches
Staatliche Museen, Berlin

This plate shows a detail from the superlative standing figure from a monastery at Dangolsheim near Baden-Baden. Carved in walnut, it retains much of its original paint.

The late Gothic sculptors, while still able to portray the sweetness and serene happiness of which this work is so outstanding an example, were beginning to find new pleasure in exploiting the three-dimensional possibilities of sculpture. The selection of less austere and more human models combined with traditional skill give pieces such as these their very natural quality.

PLATES 20, 21

Our Lady of Compassion

German (Württemberg); c. 1480
Height: 53⅛ inches
Ehem. Staatliche Museen, Berlin

This slender limewood Madonna from Ravensburg by a master from Upper Swabia (perhaps Friedrich Schramm or Michel Erhart) still has its original paint. She wears a clinging robe which falls in a few large and clearly defined folds. Her oval face is framed by a veil of russet chequered with white and draped in a crescent-shaped fold. Each hand grasps her golden cloak, and within its blue lining huddles a group of the faithful who have sought her protection. This aspect of the Virgin as a feudal protectress became very popular as a cult in Germany at the end of the Gothic period.

PLATE 21

Our Lady of Compassion

See plate 20

PLATE 31

Virgin and Child

German (Nuremberg); c. 1515
Height: 8½ inches
Victoria and Albert Museum, London

This exquisite boxwood statuette is undoubtedly by the hand
of the master Veit Stoss. Like other of his creations this
statuette is full of boldness and energy. Striking naturalistic
features such as the ugly protruding ears of the infant Christ or
the elaborate stylization of the angular folds of the Virgin's
robe are in strong contrast to the earlier studied elegance. The
big ear-shaped fold is also typical of this contemporary of
Dürer. Here on his own initiative he has created an intensely
intimate private devotional sculpture of great individuality
which shows the spirit of the Renaissance.

PLATE 32

Death and the Maiden

French; c. 1460
Height: 5¾ inches
Bayerisches Nationalmuseum, Munich

The subject of this ivory pair, like that of the "dance of death" so popular at the time, refers to the transitoriness of life. Particularly in Rosary beads on figures such as this we find reminders of death, a contemplation no doubt encouraged by the frequent plagues and epidemics. The cool elegance of the carving suggests that the artist was a member of the courtly Paris School in the second half of the century.

Dagger hilt

French (Paris); 1st half of 14th century
Height: 5⅜ inches
Victoria and Albert Museum, London

Here the skill of the carver is used to decorate a small weapon, whose hilt was fashioned out of ivory. The conveniently shaped hilt has, as a protection against a sliding blow, four heads at its corners; two of the heads are female and two male, and their symbolical function was no doubt to provide the user of the weapon with the greatest possible amount of protection.